Colson, Theodore, 1935-
  The beauty of it

(Fiddlehead poetry books ; 291)

ISBN 0-920110-89-4 pa.

I. Title.   II. Series.

PS8555.048B43   C811'.54   C80-094093-8
PR9199.3.C645B43

THE BEAUTY OF IT:
POEMS FOR TUESDAY NIGHT

by
TED COLSON

Fiddlehead Poetry Books, 1980

These poems were all written for those who met Tuesday nights at the icehouse at U.N.B.

Contents

- 7 The Beauty of It
- 8 Christ the Flesh
- 9 November Moths
- 10 Inch Worms
- 11 Dominion
- 12 Hastening through the Darkening Wood
- 12 Wind, wind
- 13 Spring, The Side Hill Farm
- 14 My Wife Stands Looking out the Window
- 14 Theory of Maps
- 17 Nuthatch Rhyme
- 18 The Counterplot
- 19 The Cellar
- 20 What Chapel Is This?
- 22 The House of Chester
- 23 The Players
- 25 The Field Where He Mowed
- 26 Lady Bug
- 27 Through Dark Trees I See the River
- 28 The Brushy Stream
- 28 A Snapshot of My Daughter and a Salmon
- 30 Of Surface and Depth
- 31 On Returning to the Church Pool on the Nashwaak River After Two Years
- 32 Hieroglyphs
- 33 The Jumantsubo Plain: A Print of Hiroshige's
- 34 Bird-Woman
- 36 Return to Gregory Hollow
- 37 Geneallegory
- 38 Professor
- 39 Spindrift
- 40 Western Journey
- 42 Two Presences
- 43 While the Surly Boy Changes the Oil
- 44 To A Lady
- 45 Near Quoddy Head
- 47 Teddy Bear, Teddy Bear

48 Ice Birds
49 Listen
50 Winter Journey
51 Old Man in the Rain
52 Easter
53 Sleeping at the Dump
54 Like a Bottle Shattered on the Cliff in the Sun
54 Encounters
56 Neighbors
57 Tramps and Boy
58 Where Was I?
60 Resonance
63 Advent Day 1977
65 The Occultation of Aldeberon
66 Moonlight, Icicles, Petals
67 To Christ In The Andromeda Galaxy
68 The Embarkation
69 Not the Introduction, But the Afterword

The Beauty Of It

Sniff, sniff in the dewy grass,
The hound tests messages as they pass.
In the course of a windy, sunny day
Scents and hound pass away.

In the course of a windy, weathery year
Grass fades, and friends disappear.
Generations come and go
And rest beneath the gentle snow.

The earth shall fade beyond recall,
The sun shall into darkness fall.
Consider all you don't understand,
And touch, touch your love's firm hand.

If she has left you unutterable grief
Cling to the sunlight on every leaf.
It's not for life's lasting that we love it;
Fragility is the beauty of it.

Christ the Flesh

Christ the Flesh
And Christ the Word
And oh the worm in my leching and lying
Sweet flowers blow
And night breeze blossom
Christ! the ache in my arms.

"I believe"
But flesh flourishes its idolatry.
Sweet lady, when she flowers in the night
Christ, I have no care of you.

I could have no care of you,
Except that your body's Resurrection
Is in my words, Word.
If you are Love and Truth, and I say truth,
My unseemly words become you.
For no true word is not flesh
Of your body.
And that leching love I stammered
Which she, my goddess, thought only lying
My God, was you.

Christ the Flesh and Christ the Word
Bread and wine and windy weather
When I lay me down this night
Blossom
And still whisper.

November Moths

Thin sunlight on the withered flower,
Thin whispers in bare branches —
Life has withdrawn
With the flocks across the marshes,
With the mouse beneath the dead leaves.

The white moths of November, erratic
Quest without question
Through the trees' tangle
And the shadow below the bank.
Their patterns, flutter, fall, and flight
Have no pattern.
Were it a wearying miniscule lust,
The entomologist comprehends.
They are not scholars;
They are fragile flights against the unknown
And unknowing shadow
Before they slumber in the frost's crystal.

All life is such
And all thought.
Profoundest logic flutters in the shadow beyond the precipice;
Blood sodden histories
Wing down and nestle in the bark's crevice.
All prayers rise, and fall, and rise
Motes in a November vista.

Inch Worms

Quarter inch, then inch
Inch, inching inch worms
Become crunching fat worms —
Glutton ugly eating all leaves,
Dropping tiny gobs, themselves
Looping dropping lobs, air weaving, worming.

When I was a boy blackberrying
Deep under the cruelest tangle
Hung greatest clusters shaded
What tropic fruit richer, more various?
But the grotto's secret was
White moths
Silver laced.
Goddesses.
I a bumbling Acteon, already beast.

Then I believed.

Saw as through Nautilus glass
The world of faerie.

Never to be denied, that world, by our world's obscenities.

Now —
From such monstrous foetuses
Larvae. Larvae.
Unfold
Sensate petals
Bloomed with living silver.
Myriad
Moths
Spangle the night.

Dominion

Where once a cloud of moths —
One alone — and this November.
The blackness surrounding is total —
There is just the streetlamp's inverted dome
And the few leaves fluttering on the trees
And wet sprinkled on the ground,
Startling bright, and small.

One moth spiraled upward   four times
And fell.

Then was gone —
In its place the occasional leaf, or shower of leaves.

I am too weary to write to its strong fragility,
My arms are ponderous, my forehead is a weight.
I would not have troubled to mount up so.
I would not be sentimental;
It was not driven by courage or passion.
Whatever drove it against November night?
Not any fate or necessity.

It was its self, frail, frail in that black night.

A gust of cold rain lashes my window.

I cannot put it out of my mind
How it seemed strong.
I cannot put it out of my mind
For four moments it dominated the night.

Hastening through the Darkening Wood

Hastening through the darkening wood
In November, cold and dark merging down,
I am startled, shocked,
By a feathered force
Silently, silently, erupting before my heart,
A great owl drifting, flickering, shade among shades,
Into shadow.

Why is it that I saunter now, bemused?
Haste has bled from my arms and feet.
I cannot remember what my hurry was.
These woods I had thought alien
Have ever been my deepest home.

Wind, wind

Wind, wind,
Off the frozen mountain
Whistle in my icy eaves

Wind, Wind,
From beyond the seven islands
Churning the grating ice pack
I cannot stop
Your whining on my frosted window

But wind from the barren lands
Twisting from the dark pole,
I stuff these cracks around my door

Black wind from the vasty holes of space,
Oh do not penetrate
To my deep cellars
Where the mice sleep behind their hidden stairways.

Spring, The Side Hill Farm

Sunset's last light suffuses its last glow
On the weathered house and barn, on bark and boughs;
It burns a slender green in the new leaves
And in new grass in the midst of the rutted road.
But shadows brim in the ruts, lengthen and flow
Down the bank, and rise in the furrows newly plowed;
Twilight eddies in the valley, forms mist, and weaves
It with the robin's song in the darkening wood.

The four great work horses from harness loosed
Now break into great galumphing gallop
Through the barnyard, toward the high rocky pastures.
They stream up the lane, pound over the road, and burst
Among the apple blossoms, up, up,
Their chestnut sides flame, dappled dashing among the orchards.

My Wife Stands Looking out the Window

My wife stands looking out the window
At deep green pine branches.
Snowflakes drift down
But a beam of sun slants through.

She is wearing a long black dress
Printed with large flowers of all colors.
As she turns toward me
Sunlight glows through the flowers.

Theory of Maps

My wife's a map librarian
And I said to her, I've got a theory of maps
That'll put you on the map, librarian-wise.
"Oh?" Skeptically.
Yes, a sexual theory of maps.
"I think that's sick," she snapped.
There went her chance.

You see, sitting on the front porch
Map exploring for salmon rivers
Shadows of branches branched across branching rivers
And I saw
Just about everything in nature branches.
A map of New Brunswick is just a mess of branches.
Now a literary map, say of Middle Earth
Or Treasure Island
Leads to a centre, Mount Doom, or the treasure.

Maps are for getting someplace
Among all the branches on a New Brunswick map
Fredericton's the centre of the universe.
So what? We all know that.

Somewhere a rapids runs
Into a deep pool
Where lies
The ultimate salmon.

The ultimate treasure chart
Guides through the treacherous forests, mountains,
Swamps and floating islands
To the great dragon and his hoard,
But beyond the beast is the rock
And there is chained the lady
And in the lady is the centre.

Think how our interior rivers, blood, lymph,
Nerves' electric rivers
Branch and branch
Lead to heart and brain and then branch out
And we branch out arms legs toes fingers
And our senses reach out
Like branches among branches
Like veins and arteries' capillaries intermingling but never joining,
Like man and woman embraced, interpenetrated branching together,
Like mother and wombed child's bloods intermingling,
Not joining, yet joining.

And after all these turnings, turn and turn again,
The wrong trail in the mountains,
The hesitation at the river's forks,
Here is the centre,
Cynosure.
Mount Venus.
Holy of holies.
Now does the shekinah dwell
In the lost ark of the tribes?

Or in the jeweled flash of the salmon, as I watch from the rock?
Or in lightning death embraced in the lady?

A map is one thing. The bush, an alder swamp is another.
The map is creased and torn, disintegrating in the rain,
Abandoned, returning to leaf mold.

We cannot do at all, at all, without maps
If
In our brains' tangling synapses
Our lives were not mapped
We would be in an infinite alder swamp
Or lost in a blizzard.

Once when I walked out onto the middle of the Saint John
          in a blizzard
My eyes were shattered with whiteness
The only stay against terror
A thin line of drifting tracks.

Maps have two forces:
Centrifugal branches leap out,
But we must have the thread through the maze
That leads back from the Minotaur
To the lady, the true centre.

Even unto
That unmapped
Map librarian.

Nuthatch Rhyme

A flash in the corner of my eye; I turn to spy
A nuthatch hanging underneath the bough
And flickering through branches heavy with snow.
Then through the trees a crazy flow,
A stream of upside down birds. Whoever saw
A flock of nuthatches anyhow?
And anyhow is the way they go
Hopover slipover find cover, half slide
Sidewise, trunk side, bark side, down slide.

Now right side up goes the life of prose
And on the whole, that's okay,
But now and then we feel all this might be transcended
And a great transcendental poet's way
Was to have it all upended.
With Emerson, and the nuthatch, a pause, sagacious
Might for the poetic view be efficacious.
I look between my legs and see
The nuthatch's world looking back at me.

The Counterplot

I found myself in this strange city, feverish
I hate its piggish crowds
But I fear more the night's empty shadowed streets
Somehow I got this basement room
At the end of the squalid hall.
By my bomb they will know me.
It accumulates in the far corner
I have tinkered it into a presence
But the powder has begun to glow like a banked fire.

It is very late
Chill drafts pry round the filth webbed window
The pliars clatter from my numb fingers
The furtive bastard in the next room wakes
And bumbles to the crusted john across the hall
The draft of his door pulls mine half open.
Nosey swine.
I quickly close it. Twist the lock.
And stare at the cracked paint and grime.

The glow has spread, and there's a little crack of fiery red.

What am I doing here?
What am I doing here?

The Cellar

I should have racked my wine, all, long ago,
So down to the cluttered cellar I go
And syphon each demi-john carefully,
Tasting red grape, crab apple, black currant, apricot.

Amidst the crevices of stones and plaster
And streaks of dirt left by the flood, I watch
The spiders weaving their careful webs —
Tasting black currant, crab apple, apricot, red grape.

Watching the glowing liquids pour
I tilt against canned goods, window screens, broken chairs;
The quiet spiders watch from their tilted webs —
Tasting apricot, crab apple, red grape, black currant.

The furnace hums, the hidden cricket sings;
I lilt among old boxes, canned goods, broken chairs,
And the merry spiders spin their dippy webs —
Tasting red grape, crab apple, black currant, apricot.

What Chapel is This?

Approach the bluff above the bay —
Short, rude stones assert timeless gaze
Among long grasses
Swept unceasingly by wind.
Look closer —
The stones are arranged
And have once been effigies —
Of men or beasts or gods we cannot tell;
The wind has wrought them to an elder mystery.
The path winds round the edge
Back to the chapel door.
A bent old lady climbs the hill from the cottage
And admits us, with authority.
She is gracious,
But startlingly, though we are too polite to notice,
Bewhiskered fully with fine white down.
I enter, after my wife and the motley group of tourists
And we are startled by
The airy room's resplendence.
In my eagerness I start ahead of the rest
And
    on the uneven floor
      of broken bronze faces
           stumble
  To my knees.
It is
  after all
    a church
And behind me the company
Hesitates, confusedly
But without embarrassment
Kneels.

When I rise, the rest do.
What   did we   pray?
It was inarticulate.
And beyond orthodoxy.   Any orthodoxy.
The stones   Compelled our blood.

The guide
The only crone I ever saw
Has summarized the known history
    The unknown is greater.
    Oh, I am troubled by a strange malady
I feel drunk, though I have not been drinking
My hands part the air
    I stand on the headland
And gaze on the ruins on the far shore
A little girl is walking up the path
Followed by a dog, a Scottie,
And her parents. Solid. Real.
But wraiths, wraiths
    Three.
Are pacing solemnly
The higher footpath.

The troubled, gaudy tourists go together
But troubled I have seen among them
Stone figures in a formal dance
The flat bronze burghers rise formal and stiff
They wear strange garb, diaphanous but gaudy
The tourists' chitchat has commingled with a chant
The chapel bell is tolling in the tilted sky
The separate surrounding grasses choir

These presences   These presences.

The House of Chester

The houses of Chester praise God,
Flourish upward and outward, like trees, like fountains.
Their timbers in intricate patterns
Put forth carved corbels
That bloom into flowers, or strange faces.
They tendril into casement windows,
Move out in windows round or angular,
In the interstices of white plaster
Form crosses, X's, shapes like aces, clubs, diamonds
And coats of arms.

They bloom in the colonnades of the Rows,
That rose out of the rubble of Roman streets.
What merchants are like unto the merchants of Chester
For their dwelling places praise God.
On Northgate Street
Atop the clustered wooden pillars
Small wooden statues in bright green
Above wooden flowers, red and white,
Wield banners with devices:
"The king himself is served by the field,"
"The profit of the earth is for all."
And houses and stores bear witness;
Over the Romani Kitchen Ware Shop in Watergate Street
The white plaster   shapes intricate rosettes, great snowflakes,
And letters, white on black, proclaim
"God's Providence Is Mine Inheritance."

Walk the top of the city wall
Above Park Street toward the River Dee —
One housefront delicately unfolds in carved faces, flowers, birds,
And on eye level, here, across the house
These words:
"The Fear of the Lord Is a Fountain of Life."

The Players

Beneath the hydrangeas and lilac bushes
Becky and Kathleen are playing house.
In the back yard the boys are shooting.
On this great stage of fools
Lear is raging.
And was there ever a Thebes
Where Oedipus revealed eye sockets bleeding?
While violins are shaping
Towers and precipices of sound,
While the defence takes the winger thudding into the boards,
At the den's mouth the cubs are tumbling.

Players.   Players all.

We have dreamed past wit of men
To say what dreams they are.
And yet the real is
The morning news of a child beaten to death,
The terrorists' shots, the famine's gripings,
The sharp word, the twist of anger in the stomach.

Oh playwright, what have you crafted?
At how many removes from the real
Are Lear's fingers groping at a button?

Don't get mad.   It's just a game.
The old coon laughs at the frantic hounds.

The hockey player slashes —
Fool!   Don't you see you've lost
The *game*.

Like a central piece of the puzzle —
There is a hole, a jigsawed shape of nothing
In the centre of the landscape.
Gone, it looks a key to that world
Vacuumed up with gobs of dust and thread and an old apple seed.

If games were really lost,

Swept out of the attic with other broken toys,
Bulldozed under garbage at the dump,
If the sea choked up, and the earth faltered,
And galaxies wound down,
Universes turned slower and slower,
And stars tumbled this way and that to nothing —

Well, we'd just have to make up new games.

Anne Frank pretended to dignity
While Hitler preened in his sweet role.
We all play roles, till the roles play us.
Don't get mad.   It's just a game.

Jesus played a role.
I bet he was surprised how far he took it —
Even though he saw it coming.
It must have been hard playing, with nails through your hands.
That was a hell of a game.
It must have been even harder
Willing back from hell and death,
Getting out of those grave windings with those hands
That this play must go on.

Becky and Kathleen squeal
Sliding down the snow bank.
The boys are digging a tunnel.

The Field Where He Mowed

Where the row of old apple trees
Meets the edge of the pines
Moving from bright sunlight into shadow
My father swings his scythe
Into the dew drenched grass
Scattered with daisies and devil's paint brushes.
The grass is dry in the sun filled center of the field,
But where light has just spilled from tops of the pines,
Where the grass is sparse, next to the shade,
Dew drops glint and quiver in the spider's web.
The blade is black with age and grime
But flashes silver on the honed edge
As it swishes the long grass down
In ordered arcs.

I stand in the doorway, shading my hand against the sun;
His old straw hat rhythmically dips.
Morning July shimmers across the acre between us.
But there is more than an acre;
Age and youth.
And yet, I feel his blood pulse in my veins;
I know the smooth wood of the handles
Swinging in my grasp.

My father is dead, and partakes with the sods.
I am middle aged, and in another country.
And the field where he mowed
Is deep shaded.
Where his eye laid the grass
Black roots of pine
With white streaks of pitch
Are firm in the rust-needled floor.

Lady Bug

I have been reading about the entropy of the universe,
How it's all running down to death,
When a lady bug interrupts me.

Ladybird, ladybird, fly away home
Your house is on fire and your children are gone,
An old charm to be said
Since it's bad luck to kill a lady bug.

A friend to man, they eat aphids.
Some places farmers go into the mountains to collect them.

A curious name:
Our Lady's bird.

She settles on my finger,
Spreads her orange shells, which glow translucent in the lamplight,
And unfolds surprisingly long delicate wings,
Then whirls in a crazy looping flight,
And daintily pulls her wings back in again.

Emerson said to the rhodora
Beauty is its own excuse for being,
But Burrough's Naked Lunch serves up
An egg containing a nasty object, an orange containing only a huge worm.
Once, on K.P., I went to clean behind a cupboard
And found about a thousand big cockroaches swarming.

Baalzebub, Baalzebub,
There are sights
That almost make us suspend our decision about
            the propriety of devil worship,
And the expediency of conciliating the devil.

I have been reading of sharks.

But the funny lady bug
Interrupts
It has no message from Our Lady
And yet Our Lady interrupts
For contemplation of a small, odd perfection.

Lady bird, lady bird, fly from my hand
Tell me where my true love stands
Uphill or downhill or by the sea sand
Lady bird, lady bird, fly from my hand.

Through Dark Trees I See the River

Through dark trees I see the river.
Autumn leaves glow
Turning in black water.

All day the soft rain falls
As I cast at Fraser's Pool.
In the afternoon a salmon leaped
just where the bubbles and little flecks of foam
slowed out on the black water.
I cast there
and had a strike
And on the third cast after that
my line tightened.   I felt its weight
And then it was gone.

Great silver sided might have been
Bearing all my might have beens
Swim in your dark caverns
While I watch the rain
And the tamaracks, yellow against the dark spruce,
Receding down the Nashwaak Valley.

The Brushy Stream

The sound of many waters
And the wind warping,
The small willows' red roots at the brink,
The rush around the old boulder turning
And tumult slowing in to the long
     Deep
          Pool.
My heart turns and turns again
Toward that day.

At the end of the pool the stream goes
    to the right and drops in a tangled rush
Tangle of roots and water and branches and sky and rocks tumbling,
And swirls — deep —
Around a great barkless high stump.
Just above that a branch of a sunken tree
Thumps softly, wetly, without end.

Hemlocks are there, low, and dark,
And the bank is cold with dead leaves
Turning to earth.
Across, the bank is high and sun warm.
There will be violets soon.
But here there is ice beneath the dead leaves.

A Snapshot of My Daughter and a Salmon

That three year old
Was not immortal. She stood there
Fixed in sunlight for a moment.
The salmon we ate
Still swims strongly deep in the ancient Atlantic.

My daughter,
Who sleeps. Or shrilly storms
Through the lives of her diminutive friends
Or drowses in the fold of my arm
Or tears at my brain when I just want to be left alone
Where is she?
And I gaze at a photograph, snapped for the sake of that salmon
Swimming mysteriously in God knows what caverns
Or channels carved deep in the mind of the sea
And I see a quizzical, half afraid smile smiled once,
Those stubby sunbrown fingers clutched once
On that alien undying flesh.

The salmon is millions at one birth and rebirth
But she in each breath expires
And changes
Commonplace is her infinite variety
She reaches breath by breath to leave me.

Oh, Amy, you brat, destroyer of time lost to your trivia of play
I loved you the moment I saw your red newborn face —
You move in my hand like a kaleidescope,
Every breath that you take
Brings you closer, Takes you further;
I can see your mind blossoming, come closer to my complexity and grief,
I can touch your mind's reaching beyond me.

She sleeps, plunged into God knows what violent child's dream
Every breath her mortality and mine.
That salmon we tried to incorporate to our blood
Plunges and slides in the inexplicable Atlantic beyond the Seven isles
Immortal in his kind
But I fall to death
With the gentle up and down of a child's blanket.
Amy I plunged you to life
Unwittingly some while ago.
Little friend, your fingers in sleep clasp mine
But cannot hold me
Every small breath that you take
Is pushing me beyond the last island.

Of Surface and Depth

Surface beauties — God! their plenitude.
I do not much need to dive or delve.
But I cast a line sometimes on the pool
To lure from the depths a fish glowing and firm,
And I eat him.

And someday old Leviathan's gonna get me.
Then I'll get to the guts of the matter
And get a Jonah's view of the rock ribs of the world
And the inner workings of constellations.

But I can wait for depth,
And now only profess
The solid strength of my wife's embrace,
The sweep of the pine branch against the sky,
The spring of my rod in my shoulder and wrist
As I cast a long line on the deepening pool.

**On Returning to the Church Pool on the Nashwaak River
After Two Years**

I meditate upon a silent theme.
The gold translucence of the sky
Filtering the turbulent waters
Reflects from the salmon's golden eye.

I trudge the dusty path through yellow alders
Through unfolding curtains like a dream;
I pause above the still and widening waters
And shade my eyes, and long and patient, try
To pierce the flickering recesses of the stream.

Across the long dry reaches of the stony beach
Heat shimmers, lonesome, lonesome as the cry
Of a long-legged shore bird in the shallows.
I meditate upon the turning leaves;
I put a question to the river
And wait against the Autumn for reply;
Sun pierces the water's deep recesses
Pulsing from the salmon's golden eye.

A small cloud of fragile asters,
Flower stars, pulse from among the rocks.
Listen. Among the crannies,
Excuse for your own being, why?
All the old disasters, all the shocks
Of love unrequited and requited quite
Pulse, pulse from the bird that takes to wing
And from the salmon's eye.

Hieroglyphs

I once thought birds all sang for joy
But I'm taught scientific fact;
The bird's song and the fish's hues
Mean meanly: "My place, mine! Get out!"

I saw one oriole kill another,
A gaudy knight in black and flame —
Head like a helmet, shining, beaked,
The female followed, tremulous.

The victim twisted panicked in air
And hung head down on a thin branch.
The victor struck its eyes, and sang
That mindless liquid melody.

How operatic. So I've seen
Resplendently, the bass conspire,
And the heroine betrayed, destroyed,
Lament in lyric ecstacy.

The tenor's dying agony
Transcends all common sense and fact.
That is, his song's a hieroglyph
Of all I do not understand.

No writ, from creatures cut in stone
To technical report, explains
The hints of meaning in those songs
Within the woods, within the heart.

Perplexed, flee to McCallum Brook
And lure the dark and radiant trout.
There's healing in this atavism —
Each run, each pool, removes all thought.

I pause, the trout gleams in my hand.
Confused, I search those glowing shapes —

The warblers fill the branching woods
With colored singing hieroglyphs.

Listen. The meaning is all unclear.
And yet amid the myriad shapes
I see myself a strange figure
Engraved within fabulous dream.

**The Jumantsubo Plain:
A Print of Hiroshige's**

The great lone eagle spreads his wing
And all his glaring eye can scan
The snow swept plain and scattered pines.

Centuries and continents away
The wind sweeps up our lonesome river.

Oh, gentle raging heart
Beyond your brush and touch
To be the eagle and the space
To be that plain. That icy sea.

Here, surrounded by the falling snow
Snow falling on the Jumantsubo plain
Among the pines and wind
And over the knoll weeds and goldenrod
Snowfilled and jeweled softly pressed
Down.
Here. Amid moans, whistles unconfined
Where the trees meet the dry meadow
And the bending grass meets the stirring almost stilled water
Forming ice in the marsh grass
And then the greater waves
And then the real flowing
And the hard first serious snow hissing down.

Bird-Woman

Falling, drifting to sleep
The images coalesced.

Treading carefully through leaves, among branches
The sound. And to his right, in a tangle, in a fall of sun
The bird rose
Explosion. And there lay still a small ruffle of feathers
Muted white and beige and brown, breeze riffled

And the girl
That lurked in every cranny of his mind
Passed in that moment through the sun articulated branches.
Coalesced bird and girl in his charged sight.

Reflecting, He understands Chagall's vague bird-women,
And the Eskimos'
Or Maeterlinck's bluebird, Whitman's thrush
The artist is a hunter. And, oh, the lover
In the strange wood.

Is it not enough to saunter and see
The red berries in the moss,
The spiderweb rainbowing the shadow
The vista to the brook's light flashing,
The fern's tracery?

He sees himself a small figure in a tangled landscape
As from the eagle's eye; the woods are endless
The sunlight departing, Darkness.

Utterly alone
If somewhere the bird did not exist
Did not feed on the fern in the spruce shadow
Did not rise through the pine branches

For years he thought the partridge's drumming
Was blood pounding in his own head.

Is it not enough that her face pulses a bright photograph in the mind?

Feathers a gray smudge driven into the shattered body
Globed handful of warm entrails
Laced fern fresh in the craw
Forgive this strange love.

With herbs
It tasted of balsam, bringing the scent of the woods
To the candle lit room

"Breathe through the heat of our desire
. . . O still small voice of calm."
The wind through the dry leaves
And the raven's croak
But mostly silences
Sunlight, or shadow, as the clouds list.

Try to see with the eagle
With his vantage, pattern.
Erratic as the moth's flight?
As the snowflake's crazy flight?
Yet the snowflake has a symmetry
Like the bird's delicate bones
And the girl's, her small shoulders
Sweet wrists, small fingers
Don a gown that feathers like frost across the pane
And whirrs through reflections into the endless wood.

Return to Gregory Hollow

Here is the creek where in summer
We splashed among the minnows in the shallows
Waiting for the chipmunk in the viney wall.
And mother praised me for saving Becky
From falling into the Spring torrent
But scolded me when I fastened
The back of her dress in the snap mop
To slow her down and give me a great handle to catch her by.

Now I remember
The eagle
Floating high.
And mother in a frenzy — knowing from her youth
Stories of eagles taking off infants —
And how I ran up that bank,
Not thinking of the cow pies then.
I found Becky in the pasture
Sitting by our cow, Pansy.
Becky had never looked so little to me before.
We stumbled back,
The eagle still, still, high in the blue.

Pansy was tied to a wagon wheel set on a stake
So she wouldn't wind the rope around.
And I remember the day she came tearing down the bank
In great roll-eyed cow frenzy,
Wagon wheel and long stake, earthy damp, tumbling behind.
There must have been a bear, father said,
Come to while the day among the raspberries.

Geneallegory

Thodore	the	Lecherous	begat	
"		" Fulsome,	who	begat
"		" Flatulent,	"	"
"		" Winsome,	"	"
"		" Garrulous,	"	"
"		" Sulky,	"	"
"		" Gluttonous,	"	"
"		" Glutenous,	"	"
"		" Globular,	"	"
"		" Forgetful,	& he	"
"		" Hurrier,	who	"
"		" Warted,	"	"
"		" Unkempt,	"	"
"		" Shortsighted,		"
"		" Timorous,	"	"
"		" Sot,	"	"
"		" Sentimental,	"	"
"		" Impotent.		

And these were the generations of Thodore.

Professor

Profess (prŏ fĕś) v.t.   1. to lay claim to, often insincerely; pretend to.   2. to declare openly; announce or affirm.   3. to affirm faith in or allegiance to (a religion, God, etc.)   4. to declare oneself skilled or expert in.   5. to admit into a religious order.

He professes to be a professor
When will he be found out?
He professes literature, professes fictions,
Faith in metaphors, absolute illogic.
Will they be found? Found out?
They quizzed him (finding out what?)
And gave him a Ph.D. —
A mask as big as a shield it seemed, at first.
Ha! He thought.   Now they'll never find me out.
But how it shrank!
It doesn't seem any bigger than underwear, anymore.
He stands behind the lectern — carefully.

He professes religion, says the creed with the others.
God will find him out.
Professes husband, father, decent citizen.
How long can he keep it up?
He professes love, despite his rancour
And faith. Ha! the paranoid!
Yes. Well — there is a plot against him, he well knows.

The streaming sky, the wind borne leaves,
The currents of the land, as of the lymph and blood,
The sharp snouted shadow through the dark bush,
The presence in the current, in the torrent.
He professes angling —
He professes the hunt.
Oh, he will be hunted out.
Angled, angled.

God grant him boldness in that day
To frame his fictions handsomely.

Spindrift

Spindrift, spindrift,
Flecks hurled in all these oceans of space,
Flickers of light in darkness and storm.

An early morning on a quiet street —
Dew glitters in the grass,
On the tricycle in the neighbor's yard.
Order and peace reign from quiet doorstep to quiet doorstep.
Why must my heart be raging?

I do not grudge my strange occurrence —
Why I should be I
On this quiet particular street
At this moment
In all the torn rage of time.
But I have raised, board by board, a little house of order around me.
They seemed hard, solid boards — rough grain, knots, slivers —
Oh they are theories, vapors,
Jagged about and vanishing in the wind.

Love is too much for my careful rooms.
They are wracked and spent in mists.
And we are
Spindrift, spindrift,
Murmurs in the oceans of night.

Western Journey

I

We sat in the planetarium
Watching the galaxies peacefully turning
Till they were distraught by a baby's raucous squalling.
In the dim light an attendant, ever so courteous,
Shooed mother and baby out.

Lean back for a larger view of eons, light years,
While blood in your forehead pulses away your moment.
Oh I could have howled with that infant —
My infancy burns falling in a crescent,
My heart knotting to a cinder.

Attendant common sense closes his fist,
We are ushered out of this little air conditioned universe
Into weather,
Close Vancouver twilight pouring buckets,
The real sky,
Searching fingers of rain, prodding icy to the skin.

II

We drove into the mountains
Where the glaciers glisten against the sun.
The road leans down, turns round a precipice.
The world drops away forever
So that fear clatters my limbs.
I want to clutch the dripping, rocky wall,
And yet I want to turn right out,
My rightful place
To plunge forever
Turning over the tall trees,
Falling over continents and planets.

III

There is a place in British Columbia
Where half a mountain fell into a valley.
Four people were caught
Under hundreds of feet of rock.

I feel tons and tons of granite hurtling on me,
Rock now vast as the sky
Has settled, with the years' turning,
And yet my heart is horribly thumping,
No avalanche can crush my buried knowing.

IV

We returned for days under prairie skies
And through Ontario bush,
Swooping down highways past vistas of Lake Superior,
And snarled in traffic in Sudbury
By the mines' vomited earth.
Oh I have come back to the Saint John valley.

I stray distracted in the grass
Wet to my knees, earth gripping me.
The stars are floating overhead,
My chest is floating out with them,
The sky and earth are distraught
And we are whirled about by their motion,
And we, distraught,
Are one with continental forces,
And yet ourselves alone triumphant
Weathering through,
As quiet as the dawn
Diffusing through the eastern sky
Stilling our racked blood to peace.

Two Presences

Gray dawn is diffusing into rose.
I feel your presence and your absence
Tangible as the light gathering
On bare branches of that maple
Accented against the black shadow of the cedar.

Yesterday morning, alone,
Pauline died from smoke inhalation.
Her wistful ghost converses with us all.
The last time I remember talking with her
She said love was the most important thing in life
And she said something about the value of suffering.
I cannot, though I try, remember what it was.
It was something I did not want to believe
But now I do —
Seeing at all times
Her cockeyed, whimsical upturned expression
As she searched for the right words.

Her counsel has a new profundity.

Now the sun shines so brightly on the new snow,
So warm on the bare branches
To look at it you would not think
Anxiety could so weigh down my arms.

Even in February I see red buds on the maple.
I reach high and pluck a spray for Pauline
And one for you.

While the Surly Boy Changes the Oil

While the surly boy changes the oil
I pace behind the Esso station.
Old tires, tin cans of every kind,
Contorted rusted guts of cars
Lie tumbled down the slope.
The ground is a hard amalgam of mud and grease;
An old rag melds with it like a fossil.
There is a mound of some black substance
Crusted with a white corroding
And clustered round it are sprays of flowers,
Tiny, bell shaped, white, streaked with lavender.
A plucked branch has a cinnamon fragrance,
Evanescent strength against the stench of gas and grease.
Now that I look, there are flowers everywhere —
Goldenrod I know,
Mounds of purple — something like phlox,
And is that white, Queen Anne's Lace?
And I know the thistle, purpling to white airy fuzz.
But flowers and flowers, mostly minute,
But everywhere resisting the trash,
Flowers whose names I don't know.
And down the bank beyond a stretch of cattails
A glade returning to wilderness —
Land unfit for trailer park or railway siding —
Sanctuary.

It is not just that I have a penchant for analogy
That in the corrosive rubble of my life
You, lady, flower with such delicate strength.
My world is filled
With your transfiguring presence.

To A Lady

His confusion is compounded by
Wet leaves upon the gravelly concrete,
Gray clouds scudding in the rain washed sky,
And smiling faces, hers — and hers —
Limned by the pounding blood. In the mind's eye.
A tracery of autumn leaves
Sprinkles her starry veil;
The morning stars in that clear night,
The evening stars, Venus ascending,
Are all, all in her eyes.
Confused, confused the planets wheel
Within his constellating mind
The morning is   damp, clear, and bright.
Sunlight diffused through worlds
Through worlds
Is, is her smile.

Confused, he leans his heavy brow
Upon his hand.
Night settles down.
The fireflies in the sedges' shades,
The constellations wheeling over
Are but the distillation of
Her glance.
O tell it not, O tell it not —
And yet
Singing in chorus
All his days perplex;
The meddlesome night hags too
Storm down, press down
The heavy heels of their hands on his eyelids,
Press his eyeballs within   turning on Gehenna
Gasp, gasp for light
And grasp;
He sees her smile, her spray of flowers
O twist from out succuba's clasp
Into that lightsome measured step.

Near Quoddy Head

The steps wind down through bracken and shrubs
Toward the sea, which spreads out forever
Where to? Where to?
The icy flicker behind his eyes
Importunes.
Subside a while by the broken stones.
Have they no warmth from the sun?
Rough, grainy, sun lit, lichen covered.
A gull cries far off from the headland
The sky, blue, is beating beating into his skull.

If he were a heap of bones
Crumbled in the bracken
Surmounted by moss,
The thick yellow green moss,
Covered by little green vines and red berries,
Though he were crumbling into the black soil
He would remember
The smooth of her thighs,
The glory of her coming.

Rolled about with gathering thunder
Off Quoddy Head
While the sea swell murmurs
The sky rolls and turns,
The wind quickens.
The sun, red, declines sullenly in fogs.
The earth turns, the stars roll
Days   months   eons.

Where were he and she in the tumbling atoms?
In the electric flashes in the blackness?
In the depths, in the surf?
In the rain receding beyond the islands,
In the fermenting soil,
In the herds scampering through the fields
Toward the dark protecting wood?

In the dark beast lumbering from his lair?

Did their ancestors never
Pause bemused, troubled by a vision
By the broad stream
As the raven croaked
Lifting his heavy wings
Through the fog
Settling to another branch in the great pine?

In the beginning,
God,
Old plotter, devious,
Did you foresee
Through centuries and centuries and centuries
The angler poised in the swirling stream
And fifty feet down and to his left
In the still eddy,
From the corner of his eye
The trout rising,
And the turn, the change of cast in mid air
And the fly lightly touching the water
And the jolt?
Did you foresee, old schemer,
How their eyes met once
And that was that?

Out of time, out of time
The river flows, and eddies,
Tumbles in a smooth sheen
To the dark pool below
Out of time, out of time
Together they stand and watch.

It winds and joins another river
And another,
And the sea.
And year by year the salmon come and go.

Parr lip the mayfly at the bottom of the run,
Great salmon turn for shrimp beneath icebergs off Greenland.

How long have they stood
Half way down the long stairs to the sea
Watching where the river merges with it?

Teddy Bear, Teddy Bear

Teddy Bear, Teddy Bear
In the blackness, comfort me.

My pummeled, worn, excelsior stuffing
Vibrates to your sweet skin.

Teddy Bear
My heart is breaking.

My fur is old cheap cloth. Your blood
Is dried and brown upon my paws
But oh it speaks. Most eloquent

Ice Birds

Clitter clatter the sharp rain
Pecks on the icy crust of snow
And rustles at the window
Like crazy birds, all wild.
All the night long we hear
The restless murmur.

The children are sleeping bad dreams tonight.
The icy birds are fluttering on their faces.
They gasp, and see the tall, gray man
Leaning into the windy rain
Far, shadowy by the street lamp
Wintery windery.
He is turning up the long steps from the street
Wintery windery.
The children look from the high streaked window —
What do they see
Through the icy rain?
The gray man is half way up the stairs
He tilts his head upward.
Beneath the battered brim
His face is contorted with pain —
Eyes, eyes through the rain
Wintery windery
The ice birds flutter.

Listen

Listen
Listen
Wide eyed children, afraid as icicles
Father and mother downstairs are shouting
Cracking the visible universe to fragments.
The ogre
Of Blackness
The ogre of wallpaper
Reaches
His curling fingers wide as the world —
Oh eat us quickly, quickly
We long to be
Forgotten.

Winter Journey

Rain blackens the maple branches,
Drips from the birch,
Collects heavy on the firs and spruce,
Collects in the low places in the snow
Turning the snow gray, soggy,
And here and there oozing into puddles.
Fog is wisping through the woods
Up from the hollow.

Later in the day a wind rustles,
Ice forms on the branches.
They clitter clatter, rustle lightly.

His snowshoes sink in the soggy snow.
Now a glazy crust is forming
And each step shatters it,
Sends tiny fragments skittering down the slope.

The rain has penetrated to his shoulders
Chill.
The fog settles closer
Dusk deepens
The rain continues, continues . . .

He must be going in the right direction.
When will he see the banks of the road
Slightly looming from the trees in the dusk?
When will he slide down the bank
Into the roadway
Secure at last?
Then he will not mind the rain lashing his face
Knowing that at last he will see lights
Dimly illuminating fog and rain
Far down in the valley.

Old Man in the Rain

That gaunt old man
Scrabbles up from where he has tumbled
In the rain
Lifts aged eyes toward the mists
      high in the elms
In the cold rain
Then down the hill
In rusty pirouettes
Old weathervane in the wind
He goes.

Only the hard disciplined
Can afford to be reckless
To dance with abandon
Into the hard rain
Into the dark wood
And the eddying rising stream.

Easter

See in this declivity
In the brown grass
Amid broken stones
How the bright blood
Trickles.   The earth
Is warming to receive it.
Swirl with that small hawk
The scudding bright sky
And come down to rest.
Has he
slashed his wrists
So that his fingers clutching the thawing earth
Send down tendrils
Into the bedrock?
Is this a corpse
This thing melded with the broken grass,
Dried grass, broken twigs, massed together.
He opens his eyes
It was not a bad dream
He has really seen what hell has to offer.
He has put his foot down
Into the rock foundation.
Is he lifting himself
As the frost heaves?
Now granite fibres
Are sinewed across his chest
And the heart still pumps.
Slowly he wrenches his body from the earth
And rises, rises

Sleeping at the Dump

Now the red sky transfuses
From the black tangled silhouette of trees
Little light to this rough pathway.
The great soft pulse of the owl's wing
Thuds, shudders across his vision.
Emerge from the branches, to an open field.
Some patches of snow linger ghostlike in the twilight.
It was a mistake to come here.
Try to escape beyond the next hedge.
As he climbs through the old wire fence
It leans around
And snares him.
The ancient dying apple tree twists its branches around his throat.
Old roots hurry to pull his feet into the ground.

In the night vague clouds scud in the dark overhead.

Faint dawnlight limns branches over his eyes.
He turns his head to see a fencepost and a strand of wire.
Half out of the snow
A broken amber bottle,
A blue mottled enamel teapot, gaping holes.
A rusted bed spring.

Now listen.
Blackbirds whirr and chuck melodious.
They riffle down the wind, rustle and resettle.
Cold   cold.
By his head, packed dead leaves.
One is maroon colored; its veins are fine and perfect
And there is bright green moss with little red spikes.

Like a Bottle Shattered on the Cliff in the Sun

Like a bottle shattered on the cliff in the sun
Scattering splintered shards
Into his eye
And his chest
A thousand bright images
Of her form
Are forever
In slow motion
Falling
Falling.
This is the sun shower
Of all his days.

Encounters

My study is in the attic.
I have a Franklin stove that smokes,
And a plywood shape of a great salmon.
Beneath it is an offering of dried hydrangeas.
From my narrow window I can see the river, in winter,
And neighboring elms, but mostly sky.

And books.
I have seen
In the swirling worlds
Strangest encounters.

Emerson wrote:
"I fell in with a humorist on my travels. . . .
He had a remorse running to despair of his social gaucheries,
and walked for miles and miles to get the twitchings out of his face,
The starts and shrugs out of his shoulders.
God may forgive sins, he said,
but awkwardness has no forgiveness in heaven or earth."

And Jung:
"As we approached the oasis
a single rider, wholly swathed in white,
came toward us.
With proud bearing he rode by us without offering any greeting,
mounted on a black mule whose harness was banded
        and studded with silver.
He made an impressive, elegant figure.
Here was a man who certainly possessed no pocket watch,
let alone a wrist watch;
for he was obviously
and unselfconsciously
the person he had always been."

For years I have looked in the mirror
Grimacing,
Hoping that age is making me better looking, surer.
However I pose
I see lurking
That humorist.

Yet the other day
I caught, looking from one mirror into another,
The profile of a funny little man
I wouldn't mind getting to know.
And across the deserts of my mind
I glimpsed
A single rider.

Neighbors

Mrs. Hectstrom
Lives alone in her big house.
Fred died of a heart attack six years ago.
The children are married, except for Emma,
And Emma got an apartment for herself last spring.
Mrs. Hectstrom keeps busy
In her yard and garden in the summer;
She's had the house painted twice in the last five years
And the stones in the foundation pointed.
She has the cleanest garbage cans in town.
There's not a weed in her garden.

Fred Ablemeyer lives next door.
His house needs paint
And a new roof.
He's trying to help the oldest, Joe, through college,
And Helen and Eleanor will go there as soon as Joe graduates,
But Avery's hardly out of diapers, and a holy terror.
The car is rusted right out, done for,
And the cat's just had kittens.
He doesn't know how it happened
But one night he kissed Mary Jean Barker
And his wife saw.
(He almost wonders if Mary Jean arranged it that way.)
He'd like to go fishing and forget it all
But a screw is missing and the handle of his reel won't stay on.
Moreover, the house he's working on now is just about finished
And he doesn't know if Stanhope will have more work for him.
He'd promised the pastor he'd fix the church steps
And Mrs. Wood just phoned to remind him.

One evening
(He was going to go to get some screws to fix the hall door)
He had just backed over Avery's tricycle
And he looked over at Mrs. Hectstrom
Who was inside her garage doorway
Painting the inside of her garage for the second time that year.
(She'd decided on a lighter gray.)

An hour before he had seen her sleeping in a lawn chair
A frail woman, exhausted.
How she kept at it.

They looked at each other, and said, Hi,
Then glanced away.
If they had looked longer
Their eyes would have said
That each quite understood the other
Across a distance like the Pacific.

Tramps and Boy

He had been running, running
In the woods
Ruffling and rattling the fallen leaves.
Beckie and Sue would never find him now.
By the railroad embankment he huffed
And threw himself
On a drift of leaves.
Looked up at the gray sky
And dull gold of elm leaves, and rust brown and winey oak.

Ed and Jake, Jake had the bottle,
Leaned against the autumn light
Stumbled the railroad ties a ladder
Lurching their ancient bones toward home
With no cares but for treasure —
Their eyes wayward for beer bottles flung beside the path.
They stood amazed above the sleeping child,
Assuming him dead, thrown there by the locomotive
As they often, often had been whirled by its passing
Like the leaves, like the leaves whirled up.

Old scarecrows straying
With eyes impassioned with their wine
But brains empty, dull as the gray sky
Pondering immensity from this narrow path.

What will we do with him? Jake asked.
Hal awoke and saw
Towering against the sky
Ragged monsters with gray faces
He thought he was in a nightmare and could not move
But tried
And throwing aside the leaves
Burst like a rabbit from its form.

Speechless they stared toward the woods where he went,
Awed at such fury.

Where Was I?

Where was I?
Loquacious, twisted in a storm of words
With a bemused smile
He looks from face to face.

You were in the Isles of Storm
Buffetted beyond borealis's reach.

You were crouched over a whitened, weathered log
Overcome with diarrhea
When suddenly a moose walked by
In the river, so close you could almost touch it.

You were casting from a sandstone ledge
Watching a loon anticking in the lake
While the morning mist rose.

You were walking down a railroad tracks
Stepping from tie to tie
In the hot sunlight that swelled the creosoted ties
With your hand on a woman's waist
And the feel is in your palm yet
Like the stigmata.

Tormented by insomnia
You turned and looked at the lightening window
    And thought
Where was I?If I could remember
Some strange adventure
Oh some strange land —
And I almost can —
I would have been asleep, and dreaming,
Not just lying there
Waiting.

Oh ye dews and frosts, bless ye the Lord.

You were in the hard clayey earth
Straining your fingers by the muddy rocks
Wet, wet with water from the river's rising
Creeping through the soil
Balked by the hard network of roots
Oh, grotesque,
Your fingers groping
Through the leaf mould
Into the air
Like the bright green spear of skunk cabbage.

Where am I?
At what o'clock in the morning
Is this a dark wood?
Is this a hard sidewalk beneath my feet?
Are those the familiar stores on Queen Street
In the fog?

Oh ye Light and Darkness
Bless ye the Lord
Praise him and magnify him forever.

You are in the strange land
Stranger than an Alpine world
As imagined by a Flemish painter,

You are just in your own bed
By your own wife
Waiting for morning.

Resonance

A student told me,
Echoing professors,
"None of the proofs of God's existence are valid."
Another says
"There are no intrinsic values."

I am listening
To the frost's crystals
On the grass blades
In the moonlight.
Your cold hand
Holds me to the earth —
Almost I can hear its heart beating.

Wind, Wind, in the branches,
Wind, Wind in the hedgerow,
Wind in the tall grasses,
Who do you whisper
As the frost forms?

God is
I said
A principle of order.

"How do you know?"

Is there a voice in the whirlwind?
Is there a voice in the earthquake?
What does the fire say?
Or in ice crystals creeping on the dark, still pool?
Now in the river's falls
Covered in cascades of ice
There is a murmur yet.

"There can't be any value
Unless somebody wants something."
"Man invented God
But now knows better."

I am listening for a small voice
I hear the sleet
Murmuring, rattling, whispering
Down hard on the surface of the snow.
Or, softer,
Crystals sifting down.

I hear wind in the spruces,
The dark sky scudding.

I hear the snow settling
Layer on layer
In the chasm
Of McCallum Brook.

At the top of an old spruce
Three ravens caw, and croak, and creak,
And one will fly up and hover
With a voice like a squeaking gate
And settle
And another flutters his great fingery wings.

I discover their three voices are quite distinct.
They are quarreling
But in an amicable, scholarly fashion.
What are you saying, old philosophers?

"Beauty can be
Only in the eye of the beholder."

Or in the ear of the listener?
I hear the brook roaring
Down in the valley
But here on the warm bank
I think I hear green shoots
Thrusting through cobwebby veins of old leaves.

Really, I am sitting in my study —
I hear from afar the squeal of the railroad cars at the crossing.
I hear the dog snoring in the next room.
And the clock ticking downstairs.
The wind is gusting in the cedars outside my window.

A cry of pain upon the night
Can murder all philosophy.
No doors can shut away the sound
Of sobbing from a distant room.

Branches creaking in the wind.

"If a tree fell in the forest
And there was no listener
What would the sound be?"

Spring's resinous life is bursting
Forth in flowers of green.
In flames of life against the dark
The robin sings before the dawn.

"What would the sound be
When you are dead?"

Why, I don't know.
I think of
The crunch of feet in the snow,
The sound of familiar steps in the hall,
The roar of water against my legs as I wade the rapids.

I think I will hang a wind chimes in my garden
And that will answer
Idle questions.

Advent Day 1977

Let the dumb ladder leap at the old spruce tree,
And clamber up in the cold,
Christmas lights clanking together.
Throw them with numb fingers
Against the gathering dusk.

This morning I couldn't sing carols
Through my raw throat.
Besides,
Instead of stained glass and muted gold
Instead of the texture of chasubles,
Of the fabric and fur of the lady kneeling in front of me,
I kept seeing
A man's face like a skull —
A friend whose grief nothing can touch.

Despair
Snaps like a bone.
This old bone is a taper.
Light it
And hold it against the dark.

The old year crumbles in the hand
Though still its bright images
        glow, glow —
Like the children around the sandcastle
In the fog with the sun breaking through
And the surf coming closer —
Its voice mingling with their voices.
Whisper. Old bone flare up
In this dark corner of time.

Christ, it's cold
Let's get this ladder back in the garage.
Friends are coming to dinner.
There are good warm smells from the kitchen.

The Occultation of Aldeberon

The banging shutter in the wind,
The half-moon long in going down the sky —
We lie in darkness and our dreams
Upon the painted darkness lie.

In this night that bright star
Will hide — occult — behind the moon
Aldeberon
Listen to the Wind
Listen to
        the listeners
                in the dark
Breathing soft, or breathing loud
As the stars turn their fiery cold crescents.

I dreamed
        all my students
                on a high stairway
Looking at the starry sky through a high window.

My daughter dreamed
I waked her for the occultation
But she made frosting for a batch of cookies.

My wife, who never dreams — she says —
Woke me in the night to say
What she was dreaming —
A hound padding through the trees
Snuffling the wind, amidst
The sharp shadows tangled
On the glinting snow.

My students on the high stairway
With eyes uplifted to the changing dark
Ignore my curious lecture, and observe
The occultation of Aldeberon.

Moonlight, Icicles, Petals

Now wide awake
Peer through the silhouetted tangled flowers
Hanging in the window
Past the icicles glowing, flickering
Outside the frosted crescent pane
To the high far white moon, circled,
     pulsing in the dark sky.

Shiver
And listen.
Lonesome, lonesome glitters the snow.

Old woodchuck curled in his den is dreaming this —
But will not remember.

Burn.
And touch the petals of the flowers silhouetted.
They are so soft   rough fingers cannot feel them.
Tear the petals
Flower by flower
And drop them
And fall with them.
Petal by petal
Fall.

**To Christ
In The Andromeda Galaxy**

Burn, child
Manger cradled against the eons
Your fibers fingering the flung stars wide

Little babe
The comets piercing
Your nail torn body
Your mercy flowing side

Tell me
Now
And ease my arms' aching
To hold someone
To lift you from the star sprung straw
To myself.
Ah child, child
Your outflung uncoordinated arms
Your whine, your yowl
Undo me utterly
See, see,
This glistering toy
My soul
Dangled.
Kick out   and coo
Flame, God
Ten trillion trillion light years out, out, out
And gather me unto
Your glorious
Now first focusing
Starry flecked
Eyes.

The Embarkation

Every tick of the clock is a petal
Spinning, purling off, to make up the self
Like strokes of paint, petal on petal
Wheeling like autumn leaves in the wind
As wide as the wheel of the planets
Curling down into chrysanthemum
A glory circle hazing the sun.

I cast myself forth on the water,
I turn with the leaves, with the petals on the air,
I slip into the current and tumble,
I meld with the stream bed,
I decompose in the shallows.

Every pulse of the star wheeling into my sight,
Every pulse of the blood circulating my eyes
Settles like petals under the peonies,
Like leaves under the maple,
Like snowflakes under the world tree
Stirred by the wind.

The crowds swirling on the boulevard, gaily colored
Know that the boulevard leads to the embarkation,
Some for the Styx
And some for Cytherea.
Oh see their idle limbs slow turning in the water,
The corpses caught in the log jam, or cast up on the sand bar —
But we fend clear, and now in the estuary
Set our sails, fleet on fleet
Like the morning stars singing together.

Not the Introduction, But the Afterword

I can tell you,
I am — well —
Ashamed of my children.
We brought them up in the Holiness church,
But they all turned Anglican.
I love those who are on welfare
Just as much
As those that support their families and drive good cars.
I introduced them to you, smiling.
But there is that little twisting inside;
I know they are unredeemed.